D1242496

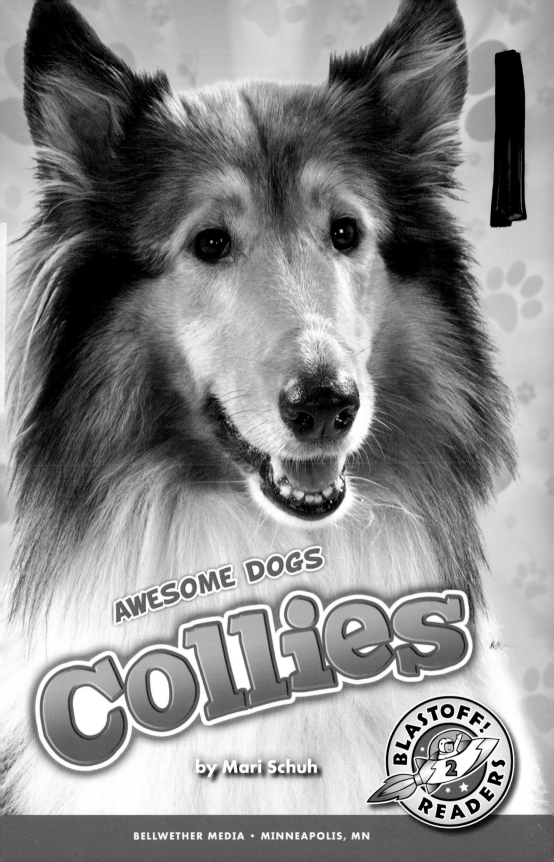

AWESOME DOGS

Collies

by Mari Schuh

BELLWETHER MEDIA · MINNEAPOLIS, MN

Note to Librarians, Teachers, and Parents:

Blastoff! Readers are carefully developed by literacy experts and combine standards-based content with developmentally appropriate text.

Level 1 provides the most support through repetition of high-frequency words, light text, predictable sentence patterns, and strong visual support.

Level 2 offers early readers a bit more challenge through varied simple sentences, increased text load, and less repetition of high-frequency words.

Level 3 advances early-fluent readers toward fluency through increased text and concept load, less reliance on visuals, longer sentences, and more literary language.

Level 4 builds reading stamina by providing more text per page, increased use of punctuation, greater variation in sentence patterns, and increasingly challenging vocabulary.

Level 5 encourages children to move from "learning to read" to "reading to learn" by providing even more text, varied writing styles, and less familiar topics.

Whichever book is right for your reader, Blastoff! Readers are the perfect books to build confidence and encourage a love of reading that will last a lifetime!

This edition first published in 2018 by Bellwether Media, Inc.

No part of this publication may be reproduced in whole or in part without written permission of the publisher. For information regarding permission, write to Bellwether Media, Inc., Attention: Permissions Department, 5357 Penn Avenue South, Minneapolis, MN 55419.

Library of Congress Cataloging-in-Publication Data

Names: Schuh, Mari C., 1975- author.
Title: Collies / by Mari Schuh.
Description: Minneapolis, MN : Bellwether Media, Inc., 2018. | Series: Blastoff! readers. Awesome dogs | Audience: Ages 5- 8. | Audience: K to grade 3. | Includes bibliographical references and index.
Identifiers: LCCN 2016057463 (print) | LCCN 2017015766 (ebook) | ISBN 9781626176126 (hardcover : alk. paper) | ISBN 9781681033426 (ebook)
Subjects: LCSH: Collie–Juvenile literature.
Classification: LCC SF429.C6 (ebook) | LCC SF429.C6 S38 2018 (print) | DDC 636.737/4–dc23
LC record available at https://lccn.loc.gov/2016057463

Editor: Betsy Rathburn   Designer: Kathy Petelinsek

Printed in the United States of America, North Mankato, MN.

Table of Contents

What Are Collies?

Collies are a smart, playful dog **breed**. They are strong and active.

These large, friendly dogs make good family pets.

Collies are known for their beautiful **coats**. Smooth collies have short coats.

smooth collie

rough collie

Rough collies have long coats.
They are more popular.

Collie coats are often blue **merle** or **sable**. Both coats can have white markings.

Collie Coats

blue merle   tri-color   sable

Some collies are **tri-color**.
They are black, white, and tan.

These dogs have long noses and almond-shaped eyes. Their pointed ears have folded tips.

Collie Profile

long nose

folded ear tips

long tail

Life Span: 10 to 14 years

Trainability:

1   2   3   4   5   6

Hardest to train   Easiest to train

The dogs also have long tails.

No one knows the full history of collies.

12

Early dogs of this breed were likely named after colley sheep. The dogs once herded these sheep in Scotland and northern England.

Scotland   England

N
W   E
S

Queen Victoria fell in love with herding dogs in the 1860s. She helped make them popular.

14

People soon began keeping collies as **companions**.

In 1885, collies joined the **Herding Group** of the **American Kennel Club**.

Later, television and movies made the dogs even more popular. People still love collies today!

famous collie called Lassie on the red carpet

Collies are gentle and calm. They make good **therapy dogs**.

People can pet them from their beds. Collies love to make people smile.

agility event

Collies need to be active. Some collies compete in **agility** events.

Others love to play ball and
go on walks!

Glossary

agility—a dog sport where dogs run through a series of obstacles

American Kennel Club—an organization that keeps track of dog breeds in the United States

breed—a type of dog

coats—the hair or fur covering some animals

companions—friends who keep someone company

Herding Group—a group of dog breeds that like to control the movement of other animals

merle—a pattern that is one solid color with patches and spots of another color

sable—a coat coloring that is reddish with black tips

therapy dogs—dogs that comfort people who are sick, hurt, or have a disability

tri-color—a pattern that has three colors

To Learn More

AT THE LIBRARY
Finne, Stephanie. *Collies*. Minneapolis, Minn.: Abdo Publishing, 2015.

Gagne, Tammy. *Collies, Corgis, and Other Herding Dogs*. North Mankato, Minn.: Capstone Press, 2017.

Johnson, Jinny. *Collie*. Mankato, Minn.: Smart Apple Media, 2015.

ON THE WEB
Learning more about collies
is as easy as 1, 2, 3.

1. Go to www.factsurfer.com.

2. Enter "collies" into the search box.

3. Click the "Surf" button and you will see a list of related web sites.

With factsurfer.com, finding more information is just a click away.

Index

The images in this book are reproduced through the courtesy of: Nikolai Tsvetkov, front cover, p. 4; Visual&Written SL/ Alamy, p. 5; Pavel Hlystov, p. 6; Marcel Jancovic, p. 7; Tierfotoagentur/ Alamy, pp. 8-9, 14; Eric Isselee, p. 9 (left, middle); Erik Lam, p. 9 (right); Capture Light, p. 10; steamroller_blues, p. 11; volofin, p. 12; Grigorita Ko, p. 13; Juniors Bildarchiv GmbH/ Alamy, p. 15; GROSSEMY VANESSA/ Alamy, p. 16; Helga Esteb, p. 17; Tierfotoagentur/ S. Starick/ Age Fotostock, p. 18; Stan Carroll/ The Commercial Appeal/ ZUMA Press, p. 19; s5iztok, p. 20; Anna Issakova, p. 21.